Unbelievable Pictures and Facts About Cheetahs

By: Olivia Greenwood

Introduction

Cheetahs are big and beautiful animals. People have been fascinated by cheetahs for many years. Today we will be learning all about the wonderful world of cheetahs.

What do cheetahs drink in order to survive?

Cheetahs drink water in order to survive, although they can go a few days without drinking water and they will still be able to live.

Are there any cheetah sanctuaries in the world?

There are many wonderful cheetah sanctuaries which are situated all over the world. You will find some amazing cheetah sanctuaries in South Africa in particular. Many of these sanctuaries try to save cheetahs from extinction.

What is the name given to a group of cheetahs?

The name which is given to a group of cheetahs is a coalition.

Should human beings be scared of cheetahs?

Cheetahs are not actually a threat to humans, and humans should not be scared of cheetahs. Unfortunately, cheetahs should be scared of us humans, as humans are known to hurt and even kill cheetahs.

Are cheetahs able to climb trees?

Despite what people may think, the truth is that cheetahs are unable to climb trees.

Do cheetahs hunt in the daytime or night time?

Cheetahs do not hunt in the night time as this is when they are sleeping. They are not nocturnal animals, so all their hunting takes place during the day time.

How long do mother cheetahs raise their cubs for?

On average mother cheetahs raise their cubs for around 12 months, they put in the time and effort to teach their children everything.

Do cheetahs roar or not?

Cheetahs are not lions and therefore they are unable to roar. They do however make other noises and they can still bark, purr and growl.

Are cheetahs smart animals or stupid animals?

You may be surprised to learn that cheetahs are actually very smart animals, they are not stupid at all.

Have people owned cheetahs as pets?

For many years, owning a cheetah has been seen as a sign of wealth. In ancient Egypt, people used to own cheetahs as parts. However, today is very illegal to own a cheetah.

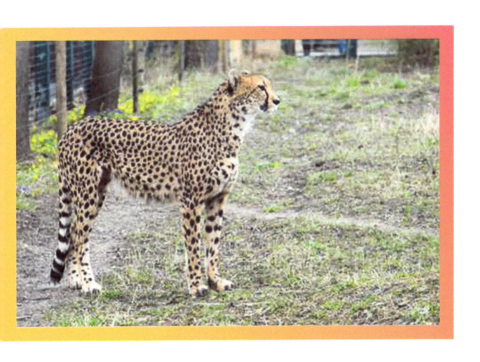

Are cheaters fascinating extinction?

Unfortunately, the truth of the matter is that cheetahs are facing extinction. There are fewer cheetahs in the world today than there were in previous years.

How many babies does a cheetah have at one time?

Cheetahs on average have around three to five baby cubs at one time.

What do you call baby cheetahs?

The name that you call a baby cheetah is a cub.

Do cheetah run fast or slow?

Cheetahs run extremely fast and they are actually the fastest land mammals that exist on earth.

How many years on average do cheetahs live for?

Cheetahs, in general, live for around 10 to 12 years at a time.

Exactly what do cheetahs eat?

Cheetahs eat a variety of foods such as gazelles and various types of other small animals.

What type of habitats do cheetahs live in?

Cheetahs can be found in various habitats. They can be found in forests, desert areas, grasslands, and even open plains.

In which parts of the world will you find cheetahs?

Cheetahs live in a few different parts of the world. They can be found in Africa and Asia. The majority of cheetahs in the world live in specific parts of Africa.

How will you recognize a cheetah?

Cheetahs are actually quite easy to recognize, they have dots all over their bodies. They have yellow fur and they also have long tails.

What is the exact animal group that cheetahs belong to?

Can you guess which animal group cheetahs belong to? Cheetahs belong to the animal group called mammals.

CPSIA information can be obtained
at www.ICGtesting.com
Printed in the USA
LVHW021927281019
635541LV00001B/103/P